BECOMING

BEAUTIFULLY ME

BECOMING
BEAUTIFULLY ME

Poems by:
Maddie Weiland

First paperback edition March 2023
Cover design and collages by Sheridan Davenport

ISBN: 979-8-218-10673-7
Contributors: Scott James

Printed in the United States of America

To my wonderful family, my courageous sister, my supportive friends, my lucky boyfriends, my groundbreaking teachers, and the princesses, heroes, villains, lessons, and many blessings in my life, I dedicate this book to each of you. You have helped me to craft my story; you have been there with me and for me in times of celebration and in times of need; you have encouraged me to pursue my passions (and I mean all of them); you have given me shoulders to lean on and hugs to make me feel seen; and you have given me the confidence to write the words I have always wanted to speak. You have believed in me — and that is a beautiful thing. Thank you for aiding in the lifelong process of becoming beautifully me.

I appreciate you more than you know.

Table of Contents

Section 4 - Broken

Section 5 - Believing

Section 6 - Breathing

Section 7 - Beaming

Section 8 - Becoming

Preface

Before we jump into poetry mode, I wanted to talk quickly about the purpose of this book and the format it's in. Since I was little, I wanted to write a book. I wanted to write a fiction best-seller that everyone loved and related to. I wanted to create a world within pages that brought the best parts of this world to life. I wanted it to be deep and emotional and make every reader think. I started my dream-book in high school thinking that was the time I was really going to do it. I think I called it *The Hidden Soul* or something like that. I was so excited to start, but when I actually sat down and got to it, I didn't make it past the first few pages to realize that fiction writing was not for me. There is just something so stressful about trying to make something up that is fun and innovative, while also maintaining your voice and telling a good story that others want to read and actually relate to. I was so stressed, and I hated it haha. I didn't feel confident doing it (and I still don't) because I couldn't understand how to do it. Like literally someone please tell me because I don't know. How does a person write a story and expect others to connect to it when it isn't real? I think I'm too much of a realist and logical thinker when it comes to my efforts to write fiction. So, I quickly shut that idea down and honestly didn't think about writing a book for years. The desire was completely gone because I thought I wasn't cut out for it— that I didn't have the storytelling gene. And maybe I don't, at least not the kind of young-adult fiction romance writing skill I was envisioning. But life surprised me (like it does a lot), and a few years after, I realized I wasn't giving myself enough credit. I could write. Frick, I knew I could write and write well because of the comments my English professors gave me on assignments and essays; the lengthy captions I wrote on Instagram posts; the full and ever-running notes tab on my phone; and the lengthy, hyper-emotional, genuine letters I wrote to my friends and family. My writing was all around me and something I noticed I did more often than I thought. What I liked most about my writing was that not only was it extremely heartfelt and genuine, but it was pretty (no matter the context or caption). The words I used were individually, intentionally pretty. My sentences just flowed, and the words just kind of melted together like chocolate. Looking back, I realized I got frustrated when I wrote something that didn't feel like a warm hug or a velvety rug or a flower petal on your hand. That just wasn't me. I found myself going back and editing absolutely everything, even my notes, to make sure it made me feel these ways. And people started noticing. I remember friends commenting on my Instagram posts that they loved what I had written or that what I said was "artsy" and well-written. I was thankful because I spent a lot of time crafting my posts to make sure my point came across how I wanted it to. I don't know when I realized that the look and feel of my writing mirrored that of poetry, but when I did, I became obsessed. Everything about my writing made sense for the first time— like ever. I no longer fretted over my style not being "fiction enough." I only cared about how what I wrote would make others *feel*. Poetry was free, and that is exactly what I wanted to be in life and how I wanted to write about my life— freely. So, I started writing more poetry and posting my poems instead of lengthy captions. Not only did the poems take way less time to write than a long caption, but I noticed I felt really proud after I posted a poem. I also noticed that I got way more comments from followers saying they really loved my piece or that they were going through a similar situation, and it was reassuring to hear they weren't alone. My poetry was reaching people— it was resonating!! So, I took that as a sign and went for it. I began writing poems about my childhood, my relationships, my wonders, and all of my many curiosities, but I also wrote about my experiences with big life changes, relationships, and growth.

Poetry was how I thought about and processed my life. It's what I gravitated towards (and still do) when I'm tossing and turning at night. It's what's gotten me through my absolute utter and complete lows and has helped me to celebrate and express my extreme highs. So, in 2021, just after I graduated college and moved to Washington to live my own life, I knew it was time to share my poems with you.

I'm at a place in my life where I feel so inclined to open-up and acknowledge some real stuff I've done and experienced that is quite frankly uncomfortable, but things I know others can relate to and be grateful that someone else experienced, too. One of the worst feelings is thinking you are alone with your emotions and shameful/not-so-great experiences, so it is my hope for this book that by putting it all out there, you can feel validated in some way, we can connect and better support one another, and together we can ultimately normalize the realities of growing up and dating and not always knowing the best way to deal with or act upon intrusive or dirty thoughts and the mess and pains it takes to becoming your own person in this overstimulated, lonely, but beautiful life.

The book is formatted into a short timeline of my life. From when I was little and naive to navigating abusive high school relationships, processing sibling dynamics to breaking up with loving boyfriends, cherishing memories with pets to experiencing unmatched love and heartache, and figuring out how to operate as a small-town, yet a worldly young woman in a new city very far from home.

This book is truly an outline of me. From birth to Washington to wherever life takes me, it's my voice, at all my ages and in every stage... and I can't wait for you to read it.
Thank you being here. Thank you for entrusting in me to seek hope and love and a confidante in poetry. Thank you for giving me a safe space to debut my poetry.

I love you. I appreciate you. I support you.

Welcome to my story of Becoming Beautifully Me :)

BIRTH

THE
BEAUTY
of

ROOT

BLIS
BETTI

The Slipper

Disney was merely more than a thought within the life she lived.
It bore, rather, the delicate shine and curved lines to each slipper she wore.
Personified mice lingered not far,
but hidden they kept in guard of her time.
The appearance of dark made her stumble,
although she lost neither slipper but one.
Mice are of magic until time is worn.
Step into her closet.
It is the believing that makes for a perfect shoe to fit and be worn.
Time and time again :)

Meet Me in Neverland

I call her Wendy.

A doll in her hands.

A green cap, too big, steadily inching down, always falling in his face, and a scarlet, frayed feather caught between knots in his wild fray of hair.

She is blushing.

A pink marker sits next to my hand, ink marks stain the floor, and pink polka dots freckle my arm.

I rename her Belle.

A book on her lap, blue bow too long, gradually letting slide, never quite keeping the hair away from her face.

He wears a red cape that's too small and slides from his shoulders and a golden, shiny pin tangled within hairs of his matted fur.

Her cheeks blush.

My mom's makeup kit lies open on the carpet, brushes askew.

Test stokes line my hand, the same colors cover my lids and pucker my lips for true love's first kiss.

I want to look like Wendy, Belle.

His brown head is bent down, absorbed in a book. His glasses frame his face, project his eyes, and hover across each word on each page.

My Peter, my Beast, my Prince,

My Neverland awaits.

Ode to Beary

The innocence of childhood
was displayed in my arms
where I carried my bear
cuddled near my heart.
his image is simple,
fur masking his eyes
his heart is pure,
disguising no lies.
His soft grey body,
always warm to the touch,
shielded me from evil,
of monsters and such.
These qualities he holds
are reflected in me,
so, an ode to my bear
who lays cuddled beside me.

Simple Times in KY (2018)

I love green grass and blue skies and little bugs that begin to fly
I love big trees and new buds.
I love fresh flowers and blooms that sprout from little stubs
I love sunsets and sunshine, especially on Saturday's
I love skirts that twirl and people~ the dancing kind
~ that dance between moments of each day.
I love sisters that giggle and little caterpillars that wiggle,
And I love moments that make me feel that the world is grand
and that the stars just beyond my reach can be opened like a treasure
chest to every explorer that adventures through this beautiful land.
I want you, each of you, to hold hands,
as we set forth to understand why things happen in life
and how we can be ~ how we are ~ strong
as long as the beautiful earth gives us a place to stand.

A Reflection on Life

My happy home with
Dancing swimming women who
Embraced our mommy :)

Hand Holding

Hey sis,
Do you remember that tradition we started
On our first flight together?

We were so little
And we held hands
For all of the "scary" moments
Of the flight
— Especially take-off —
When we would go really fast and it felt like a rollercoaster
Like when the wheels would come out from under us and we had to
put
Our mercy into the sky,
So we could fly

Do you remember that?
Or when we got older, and we weren't always seated together
We would stick our pointer fingers'
In the air— just one —
Just high enough for us to see them over the seats
To pretend our fingers were holding on to each other's,

Seat to Seat.

I have taken so many flights since, Kenz
Some of which we were together
Others not.

Often times the flights got scary
Especially when turbulence occurred
And at first, I was uncomfortable not having you there
(I remember fidgeting in my window seat
Pressed against a stranger)
And I decided to stick my finger in the air.

I did that for a while, Kenz
On every flight to Texas and Kentucky and Washington and back

It made me feel better,
Like you were there.
But it never felt enough.

This time, I decided to clasp my fingers together and wrap them tight
Pretending — Believing —
That I was holding your hand

Like I always did
In flight

And that time,
It felt right :)

Thought Monsters and Honeybees

Blankets used to scare me
Because
I thought thoughts, lots
Got lost in them,
Underneath.

Blankets used to scare me
Because
I thought monsters, stirs
Got spooked by them
within reach.

Blankets used to scare me
Because
I thought tales, got
Tattle-taled to the monsters
On me.

I got a blanket last year.
Because beliefs
Believe it or not
Got lost to me.

My blanket is strong
And heavy
And scares the thought monsters
Right out from me.
It has flowers on it
Yellow, bright bulbs with perfect dark, crayon-colored green little
leaves and a dark dot in the middle of each
(Probably where the honeybees meet).
It also has a light blue background
(that is the sky to me), at dawn when the color is pastel (I don't like
pastels) and the world waking up fresh anew.

My blanket doesn't scare me
Some others do
Some others are scared of bees
Get spooked by them, too.
So
I understand.
I thought
— I think —
Blankets still scare me
But my blanket reminds me
I am here for more than monsters
But for flowers and honeybees and even those pastels too :)

CBV

You make me weep
Remember when I used to sing you
Lullabies
Tickle you
Massage, rub your ears bumps lumps of love
Until you fell asleep?

I miss you
And I'm thinking of you
Your siren song with Nellie
Makes me weak

Rest In Peace
My sweet
Sweet
Boy
Sing for me
Breathe life into me
Until I fall asleep to dream
of you and bumble bees
Fairy wings
Butterfly bushes
Couches with cushions
Swimming pools
Chlorine handfuls

Eat the air
Bite the gnats
Be the boy in the breeze
Dance with me, sweet boy
Waddle for me
Show me how your heart is happy
Tell me what makes your heart full

I will always sing you
Lullabies
Tickle you
Massage, rub your ears bumps lumps
Love you for always
My Big Boy
My CBV

~To the best dog this earth was blessed with, see the world for me~
Sir Clyde Billy von Chester

Maybe I Can Be a Sunflower

maybe I can be a sunflower
I stand alone now
what's different from
human to
Flower?

maybe I can be a sunflower
because I don't want to fall and shrink up and cave in and shrivel
like those little petals
of little flowers
like the challenge little people
with feeble wings face

maybe I can be a sunflower
because I like independence
because I like freedom
because I like the idea of a new place with
open space
and air that's breathable and makes you want to swallow each sip
with a fervor
that so powerfully mimics grace
somewhere nurturing
somewhere safe

maybe I can be a sunflower
because sunflowers
are beautiful
and strong with a core
that defies human strength
and I like beauty,
soft face

maybe I can be a sunflower
because sunflowers yield seeds and I

like that
mere dandelion wishes
can be dreamed and achieved upon a simple seed
and run sufficiently
just me

maybe I can be a sunflower
because I choose to be something
everyone secretly whispers to behind my big green thick leaves
and admires
and doesn't pluck at to waste

maybe I can be a sunflower
because choosing defiance
doesn't mean choosing an escape
but choosing opportunity
to grow
bud
bloom
with grace.

I'm Not a Weed

I was a leaf
once attached to a tree
now torn from the fingers
of a little
kid who wanted to feel
the texture of my back
hear the crackly sounds
I make
between their thumb's friction.
I. me. my pieces were then scattered beneath the tree
My trunk.
I was crushed like pepper
not able to taste
the spice,
fragrance,
of an autumn
that once was a texture
of straw
the color
of plum ruby green.
For I was plucked
off by a pinch
that detached my steam,
littered
my body like debris.
Watching from the ground
I saw
the thumb reaching
for another,
another leaf-
one that saw me torn,
spiral down-
that grieved,
cried,
"Don't pluck me. I'm not a weed."

Privately We Sailed

Although once a sailor,
I found that I was lost at sea.
I continued to steer,
but merely in the wrong directions.
Each turn took lead me to a place I didn't want to be.

I realize now,
I never wanted to be a sailor.
I wanted to walk along the water's shore.

But I was swayed by a boat
that took both you and me on board.
The water at sea was never clear though
unlike the water near the shore
where I could see my toes
and bury them beneath the sand.
It was deep,
deep like you and me,
a hollow of murk,

private unease.

Caught

I still taste your mouth
lingering
overtop my own
Soft.
Warm.
Fierce.
I gave in and fell open
You swallowed wholeheartedly
And bit my lip each gulp.

I still hear your voice
unyielding
Each word curled around my neck
Firm.
Heavy.
Tight.
I was bound to you
And I regret.
You gave no silence to speak my words.
Swollen was my lip you bit.

I still see your body behind my lids
Pale.
Weak.
Thin.
I was caught by a hook
And bobbing
You reeled me in with faulty wire
And pulled
Puncturing my throbbing lip.
I still sense your mood play out
Insistent.
Mad.
Cantankerous.

I fed the snake its lust
And permitted myself to be taken on board.
You inclined the speed
I threw up each word you gagged me with
And massaged my bitten lip.

I never wanted to hurt
But that's all I seemed to feel.
You snake.

You monster.
You wretched lover.
I enclosed my rage around you
And bit back your lip that bit.

How I Think about Anxiety

Think thank thonk
Think thank thonk
— Faster
Think thank thonk
Think thank thonk
— Breathe faster
— Speaker faster
Think-thank-thonk
Think-thank-thonk
— Feel your heartbeat increase
— Faster faster faster (almost whisper it)
Think thankthonk
Thinkthank thonk
Thinkthankthong
Thinkthahhhhaaahhhhhh

"STOOOPPPPPPPP!!!!"

you scream out loud
The first thing you have voiced out loud in a year
Other people hear.
Other people see.

"What's happening to me?"

you can't even breathe.
you can't even think.
you don't -can't- sleep.
"I think my thoughts are becoming me."

-The Real Me

Am I a Good Girl?

I was caught in a relationship
In which I had no rights.
I was property to him
a slave is to his master.

I swallowed the sickly poison he mixed into my spit.

Your hair grew in flames
Ignited by my stroke
You were the fire,
flames to my wick.
You grew a possession
Of me, "my"
What you wanted,
And I regret.
I regret the bitter taste,
Pungent smell
You unsuspectingly gave off.
An odor that traveled too far inside me
Lingering.
I couldn't escape it remove wash scrub rub it away.

The taste of his pale skin possessed my senses.

Did you ever stop to think
That maybe the smell
Was the metallic sent
you gave my blood
Each time you bit
And bit
And bit.
No
My breath was worse,
you said.

Too bad he didn't know that all he was smelling,
tasting,
Were the traces of his sickly spit.

So, I ask,
"Am I a good girl?"
because I couldn't get off what he meant to stick?

The Intruder

the Leaf
punched
the Intruder
on the back.
he laughed
looked in front of him,
up at the Tree,
"stop mocking me."
i heard the Leaves
Crunch
Dead
as he
left.

until the next Intruder interrupts
the Forest,
I whisper my wishes
to the Wind,
let it carry
my promise
to the Trees,
Branches,
Leaves
that I will remain
loyal
to the Ground,
Growth
Above,
Beneath.
i hear a rustling in response.

a Leaf
tickled
my arm.

i smiled.
Another Leaf fell,
then Another
and Another.
I sat smiling surrounded
by love, lovely Leaves.
The Forest swayed,

waved goodbye
when i left,
careful not to step
on the Reds,
Browns,
Greens.

i turned around to wave in return,
but the rustling
had stopped.
an Intruder
plucked off a Leaf.

I Never Liked Hot Sand

I like a metaphor that could drop me off on shore.
To let me,
once again,

be Free

lay beneath the sun
and allow the sand to run

Freely

through my hands
and wait for the hour
where the sand no longer falls.

Like you and I,
the time will dry
left out too many hours withering under the sun.

I feel my skin burn,
and peel its layers.

Raw

and exposed,
my feet cry
walking back home.
There was no shade to cover the hot sand.
But I would rather walk sorely,
Then retrieve my shoes left near his place.

<u>Gone</u>

No expression
I am a match burned, unlit
Smashed to withers I feel
Always.
Always.
Take me away
Far
To a deadpan place.

Gone is the road I walked on.

My Name is Peony

At dusk,
My bud heavy,
I curl inside my pastel petals, edges torn, frayed.
Dew drops, mist, collect along my feeble, olive leaves.
A tear glistens clear,
Running smooth to drop, puddle around my stem.
Deep, I am rooted.
Unblossomed, within a dreary mood I stay.
I haven't the strength to bloom.

-

A green, deepened by dark hours,
awaits arriving dawn.
The olive tinge as an outline of my pointed, crisp leaves,
now a shade lighter,
a mellow lime in mix with jade.
Smooth, linen petals cocoon my character.
Inching high, forward, toward the sun
I adjust, stretch my roots positioned deep.
Withered, a lone and thin parched leaf, I pluck to spiral freely.
I unravel to reveal my inner bud,
blushing, fresh pink in play with the light.
Ombre.
Golden is my stigma revealed.
My stem supports life at bloom.

Triggers

So many things are a trigger because of my abusive relationship
I took to realizing this when I dated my first love
Because so many things reminded me of him
And I got scared
And I remember I would cry sometimes
Because I was so caught in my head
And I couldn't separate my reality from my emotions within

But now that I am safe
(I guess now that I have absolutely no relationship with anyone)
I'm figuring out my traumas that have been silent since

And my heart feels a little broken
Even though no one is doing anything directly to it
But that's okay
I'm acknowledging and getting through it.

BRACING

You Can't Talk in Dreams

I woke up at the time
You and I would
Fuck

I did it again
I felt myself up
Thinking
Your hands were mine
Imagining you
right there
— right here —
in my bed with my hands.
On me.

My hands hurt from all this
Thinking

No one told me
I had to think
how to fuck

No one told me
I had to imagine
a sound only felt

No one told me
I had to wake up
To a
Dream (one of those repeating ones)
Because
All this thinking
Has created a reality
Unfathomable to even me.

My hands hurt from fucking (Do you get what I mean?)

Babe,
Do you have this same dream?

Mod Podge

Loving you is hard

... I thought
I could
Collage you
Onto my arms

Mod podge you
Into my skin

Layer you
       Upon
               over
                    Every
                    layer of me

But I'm quickly learning that I can't
Because some paper tears when it's wet
And some people aren't meant to be so close to me :(

You Didn't

You didn't make fear the military.

You made me fear what I might be
If I were to allow it
To take back that part of me.

You didn't make me fear the military.

You made me fear what I might be
If I were to date a
Boy
Who lives and breathes time with his
"Buddies"

But
Doesn't get
"Leave"
for me.

I Breathe

I often hold my breath
Too tightly too hard too clenched
My stomach churns
My hearts burns,
Too. He teaches me to breathe
Lightly
deeply
Fully
Until my heart burns yearns pumps not churns
For us two
Be, breathe, together.

__Distance__

Today we talked about

Distance.

But I ask myself
Can I
Go the distance?

Again?

Collaging is like a Puzzle

I wanted to be a puzzle maker
when I was little.
it's so sad that now I stop myself
and think,
"Is that even
A
Real
Job
?"

-the doubt in my reality

A Gift

Why do I fall for
Him —
His —
Loyalty
for a job
For a life
For a body
For a dream
For everything
For everything
but me
in
The present.

I am a present
And
Sometimes
I Feel —
I fall —
Because for one second
They openly appreciate me
They flaunt me and compliment me hold me so close

But then they leave

because
Loyalty is not a gift
To us all.

~my thoughts on the military

Sick

Why do I feel like I'm gonna
vomit
when I cry?
Heartbreak is hurtful.
Heartbreak makes me sick.

Letting Myself Go

I'm scared
Like a heartbeat beating way too
Fast.
I'm scared of hurt
Hurting a heart that
Was meant to last.
I'm scared to feel feelings
I have repressed back
I am hurt.
But it's me who hurt my heart
His heart
I am sorry
So sorry.
But I have to let -letting- go of the past.

Breaking Up is Not a Fucking Joke

He was in my dream last night.
It was the first dream
He and I
Weren't happy.

He wasn't mine.
It was the first dream
He and I
Didn't smile
Didn't fuck
Didn't joke
He didn't seem like him

Because I was no longer the her
Either of us knew me to be.

My heart broke in a different way last night
(Before it was fogged glass, but now
It's a broken mass laying all over the place
In the space we lived).

It was the first dream I had of us
Since.
It was what I needed,
I guess
But I didn't smile
When I woke
Because breaking up
Is not a fucking joke.

<u>i wish</u>

I wish flowers grew in winter.

I wish flowers bloomed in snow.

Feeling Blue

I had sex today
And it wasn't with you
I wanted it to be wonderful
But it wasn't
And I know it could have never been
Because he wasn't you

and i'm feeling blue.

<u>Do You Ever Miss the Crickets?</u>

Do you ever miss the crickets?
In the dead of winter.
It's like
having thousands of best friends
Right outside
Supporting
Rooting for you
Keeping you company
when it's cold and silent and lonely.

That's what I miss in the winter.

- My friends

First Time I Loved

Hey A.
How are you?
I think about you all the time
But I want you to know that I loved every minute
of when you were mine

Some days my heart hurts more than most
Because I fear I will never find someone who knows me most
Unless someone uses a hammer to break me down
Right now
I will settle for your ghost

I have walls now, A.
I've never had these walls before
Because our love was so beautiful
To have a love like what we did
It tears me to the bone

I laid broken on my bed that day.
~
I was watching my favorite show
Today — something I started after you — and I
Learned
There are 5 types of love:

There is Unconditional love
That is beautifully taxing
because you would go to the end
of the earth for each other

There is Complicated love
That is difficult to make work
For whatever reasons
But you both really want it to

There is Forbidden love
that is all about the desire of
the chase
and the high that follows

There is Rekindled love
That can be magnificent
If the rekindling is for the best,
But heartbreaking all over again
if the circumstances don't quite fit

And there is First Love
the magical fairytale love we all dream about
that stays in our hearts'
forever.

A.,
You were my first love.
I will never forget you
Because the first time I truly ever loved
It was because of you.

- Thank you

Life Here

Everyone has a life here.
They are busy living life here.

But I don't have a life here.
I've tried to make a life here.
I've tried to make friends here.
But I don't have a life here.

And
That makes it hard
To start
living

Because
I can't seem to make new plans
With people I've met once
Because they are busy with people and plans they've met
and done a bunch.

<u>New Life</u>

I moved to Washington 4 months ago
Rainy season
Has barely just
Started.
In fact,
It's now fall.

But I already feel washed out.
I'm wet actually.
I'm waiting
-actually-
Hoping
That
Washington is a metaphor.

Like all of my English teachers have taught me my whole life
Washington better bring me new life.

BROKEN

as! It's Bananas! It's B

Cry for Hi

Saying hi makes me want to cry
a glisten in the word hi
a simple dimple
Twitch of the lip cheek
Apple of the eye
"Hi", I say
but I mean never say goodbye
Fucking love
Like me
Want me
Date me
Love me
But don't want to fuck me
Don't want to have me
Don't desire to date me
Make me want to like me for me
Make me want to
date me
Make me want to love
to love me
Make me crave to fucking fuck me.

Perfect Fault

Society is brutal like a lion,
It will tear you apart.

Let the games Begin.

News Flash:
Barbies only.
Perfects to the right, Uglies to the left
No questions asked.

Be careful.
No one's safe.

Cut back on your rations,
Unless you find stares attractive.
Wouldn't want to disturb the enemy.

Let's pause for a moment,
Or do you still need time to look in the mirror?

Forget it,
You'll never win.
Too caught up to notice the game Ended.

They won.
You lost.

They have an image
Etched into everyones' mind

But your image was repelling
And foul to the eye,
Not meeting the standards society sets.

...

Hold On:
Switch controllers.
You Restart the game.

You must adjust your standards.
Make them struggle
And watch them drown.
Erase the commentary and cruel remarks left

As their last words.

View them as nothing,
As lifeless as a brick.
And use those bricks to build yourself
To let what is "Ugly" win.

Wants vs. Needs

He wanted to fuck me
Told me he wasn't expecting to get
Laid
But he proceeded to
Kiss me
Take my clothes off
Bite my lip
Suck me
Rub up against me
Condom free.
And I said
"fuck you"
Not me.

You don't have a condom,
Leave.

An Object in my Chest

I feel like an object is
constantly gnawing at my chest

It is not suppressed.
It is not at rest.

You know what it is: resistance.
It kind of feels that an ice cube was put on my
Breastbone out under the sun
You know what it is: shock.
And all of my nerves were put to the test

The body is designed to resort back to equilibrium: perfect balance.
Bliss.
But I have never felt perfect nor balanced
Just tension at the repression
At the object in my chest

I have tried to melt this feeling {because I know that ice is an extreme of
water imbalance}
But
No matter how much time I spend exposed to the sun
The ice only seems to burn my chest.

<u>Don't Know How I feel</u>

Sometimes I don't know how I feel
When
Guys flirt with me.
A pickup line?
What is that cringey thing?
Pictures of their banana split
Boxer Briefs in the first Snapchat they send me ...
Cringey.
Is it just me
Or is that wayy too much for a
Just met
First date
First text
Talk to —
No—
Just started talking to me?

<u>Tainted</u>

I look at a
guy's Hands
to see how they would finger me

— another way
my hoe phase has
Tainted me

Fire

Today I felt uncomfortable with the situation of my
Vagina
I was in the middle of having sex with a
Cute guy —
A firefighter actually —
And then I pulled away
Because I was afraid my health could
Very
Well not be okay.

I thought I was okay, but my
Vagina
Apparently isn't because it smells
Very
Sour and sex didn't feel the best (not because of him) I'm just in my head
but I just went to the doctor, and she did a test and she said everything
was okay and for me to use condoms and I did and to prioritize my
health and I do,
And to eat lots of fruits and antioxidants,
And I am.
I am doing everything right.

So, I pulled back
I pulled out
Very
Abruptly
The firefighter said there were tears in my eyes. I lied.
Visibly

My eyes were basins of water and I sobbed, bawled
I felt
Very
Very
Very

Dejected
In my own skin.

I need this fire to be smoldered
So I don't feel like this again.

3rd Grade State

Why do guys say
Wyd?
Wdym?
Fr? Ya. Or yuh.
It pisses me off.

Talk to me.

Even a 3rd grader knows what to do with a sentence.
And they know about abbreviations.

But you fuck the guy who said
yuh
And now you're pissed off.

But wdym? He asks.

I want to go back to 3rd grade. You state.

Remind Me Why

Remind me why I shave for men.

Wait a sec, no we gotta edit that.

Remind me why I shave for men when I know they will cancel on me.

That's better.

Remind me why I shave for men when he refuses to come to me.

Oh, now we're getting places.

Remind me why I shave for men when I feel sexy and fantasize that my reality is he.

Frick.

Remind me why I shave for men, please.
Remind me why I have to remind myself to shave for me?

<u>So Nice</u>

You were so nice
And treated me right
But I want tonight to
Be
Something naughty.

How nice :)

Ring-Ring

I'm in the middle of emailing you
And an engagement ring pops up on my feed
Is it a coincidence
Or is it meant to be?

Because
I do
Love a pretty-little ring
Ring-Ring!
Call me please!

I'm in the middle of my hoe phase
And I need to know if you're worth talking to
Please.

Well, Shit

He's the one that got away
And I'm freaking sad
because we made plans
We were gonna fuck
We FaceTimed on an app
But shit
I guess he deleted that crap.

Done

I'm done with everything.
I'm numb to it all.
I no longer want to talk to guys.
I no longer want to date at all.

BELIEVING

Remember When

Remember when
We first met?

I was so happy to see you
I jumped into you—
Your arms
Your chest
Your body
Your soul—

On the elevator that night

And we climbed
To the top

Even though
We were headed
To the bottom floor

Remember when?

I thought
We would make it so far...

I like You, But I Shouldn't

I like you,
But I shouldn't
But I want to.
I crave you,
But I wouldn't
But I need to.

Tell me I'm wrong
That I shouldn't that

I
won't
Don't
Like you.

You are the reason
I like dynamite because
Of the excitement
release
dazzling explosion
of everything I have ever known
about relationships and life and god damn fucking
in love, oh not with you,
but in love with the sensation
like I've been electrified with the ability to experience in another
dimension.

But,
I thought I just liked you
I told myself I just liked you
But,
my hair is on end
Because I'm vibrating from your dynamite stands.

Break {Broken} Beaks

Breathe my breath
Please.
Kiss my neck
Please.

Kiss {not peck} the beating thought monsters {monstrous thoughts}
right out of me.
Please.

Break my beak
Kiss my cheek
Tell me the
Wood pecking has stopped
Moved somewhere else
To think monstrous thoughts in peace.

Can I Have a Hug?

When I ask if I can have a hug
I actually mean I want you to cover me up
To wrap all of your love and emotion around me
Swaddle me in your arms
Kiss me

Actually, hug me with your lips.

Next

One night he sent an
"I miss you"
Text.
He was on duty.
I was in bed.
I hadn't heard from him in days
Hadn't seen him in weeks— months it felt —
My heart sped up so fast
My eyes didn't leave the message — didn't blink —
until it left the screen.
I don't want you to be my next ex
I just wanted you to be my
next

__Tell Me__

I've lived with you
But you've never
Lived with me.
Do you ever
Wonder what that could be
Feel like smell like look like be like?

Tell me.
What do you see?
Who do you want to live with?
Me with you
Or you with me?

I'm So Glad

I'm so glad I emailed you
It's like Dear John
But Dear Jack
And not sad
But happy
Because that is the one time we got to talk again
I got to love you again
to learn more about you again
See how you've been
I miss the sun you miss the waves
You said you'd take me surfing
I said take the reigns
Let me call you a cute name
He said okay :)

Reply

My heart yearns
for him
In a way that makes me
wanna cry

I wanna say hi
But it's
his turn
To
Reply

Part of Me

Sunsets are my favorite thing
How did the world
Know
It was time
To see the thing that is most favorite to me?
How did the world
Know
To send show set sun skies
For me?
How did the world
Know
He
Is a sunset to me
And that he sets sun beams light rays
Lights up every part of me?

<u>Together</u>

It's ironic, we travel the world,
But never together.
It's ironic, never are we together
But together we are the world.

Black-Out Poetry

I want to write you
Like black-out poetry.
I want to find only the most perfect, most hidden, most unpredictable
but perfect
words to describe you
And I want them to all be on the same page so I can look at them all
together and
read you
like the best romance novel I have ever read.

<u>Butterfly Love</u>

I am on cloud 10
I am a teenager again
But this time, I am free

He asked me what I was feeling
And I smiled {I blushed actually, but he didn't see}
I feel giddy happy excited butterflies' relief connected
to him
to me
I feel free to be
For the first time
In being this new me

I want to call it ecstasy

But
It's more than that
I think I am a giddy happy excited butterfly
Blushing
And

Finally
Flying

Free :)

Sleeping with Butterflies

It's interesting
Every guy I talked to made me stay up all night with
Jitters.
It felt like butterflies were crawling out of their chrysalis'
It felt like they had metamorphosized into
Something I wanted to like
But I felt like they were surveying my stomach and my every insides.
(They felt like unwelcomed guests).

I thought butterflies were supposed to be delicate
Special
Float
Soar
I thought they were simply little beauties in the sky?

Since I've talked to you
I stay up,
But
Only to nurture the butterflies, to make a home for you
To make a home for them
(so they no longer feel unwelcome in a place I love most)
:)

<u>Something to Wake to</u>

I want to wake up
to the sounds of birds
go to bed with
bugs and beetles
and wet grasses, fresh dew

I want to sing a tune
{Even though I cannot sing a beat}
something sweet, chirped
Hummed, whistled
Loud
or soft
light
but right, just right.

Tickle me
With goosebumps
Cause every drop of fresh dew
To smile at
me and you
Wake me up with
All of the nurturing nature
of wanting to
want you

A Bonsai & Me

We talked about getting a Bonsai tree.
Maybe that will be the day he'll marry me.
Grow our love with our little tree.
Water him each day.
Our anniversary

Eternity

I'm obsessed with you
With the way your smile reveals hidden dimples
And the feel of your hair on my cheek
And the way we snuggle

Equal parts you.
Equal parts me.

I'm obsessed
With the fact that we hadn't seen each other in four months
Because that made our meeting even more of a treat.

I'm obsessed
With the way I saw you run to my apartment
Watch me struggle to open the door
And give me the biggest bear hug that
Picked my heart off from the floor
As we stood in the elevator doors.

I'm obsessed with you
Because I met you today (a soul I have known for years,
but somehow never could see).

I kissed your smile and your dimples on your cheek
I touched you in places only a pure soul can be
And felt your heart press against mine (merge into me)
Inside
Outside
Underneath
On top of me
And in knew in that moment
I never wanted you to leave
…

Can we stay this way for eternity?
Please?

Wanting, Waiting, Wishing

I've never wanted something more than a reason
For more than a reason
That something is you. <3

Stop-Motion Pictures

This email chain is like a stop-motion picture.
Every message is a picture
But there are so many rough
Chopped
Up

Fragmented

Spaces

in between
Send

-Sent-

And
Received.

Fleeting

Time with you is

fleeting.

1 message here and I don't hear from you there

But then
Out of nowhere
He says,
"I miss you I hate texting I just want to see you"
And I ask,
"What do you miss about me?"

"Everything," he says.
"Literally everything."

And my heart skipped a few beats
Because I knew this moment
was

fleeting.

Motorcycle Man

That was unexpected,
that whole night was unexpected
and, shit,
I really enjoyed that kiss.
Thank you Bumble for
bringing me this :)

Serendipitous Jeans

"The man of my dreams"
sounds serendipitous.
Jeans I want to dip my hands into his back butt-cheek
pockets and grab at to
squeeze ;)

<u>Fiji Babe</u>

If Fiji is a fantasy
I'd like to go there with you
Dive into the waters
Blue aqua
So, babe
Baby blue

Me and you
A hut for two
Babe, feel my fantasy
Isn't it fantastical?
I'd like to go there with you.
Be my Fiji—
Be my babe, baby blue.

<u>Boxer Briefs</u>

I was in his boxer briefs
With me underneath
Wearing just enough
of me
With his skin
On me :)

Bumble Bee Love

I can't wait until you and I will
never bee anything but
a part of never ending
happy endings
bumble bee love

Fuck You

If we make us
Happy
Isn't that the only thing that
Matters?

I poured my heart out to you
And now it is
shattered

I'm so confused
Your demeanor stayed true
So, thank you
But your vibe was
Not the happy-go-lucky you

I don't care if you don't want to do distance with me
That's not it at all

I just don't understand how you kissed me so passionately and giddily
laughed with me
as I jumped back into your arms
before realizing backing down
Ditching us
Ditching everything we could be
Was the right thing for
We

I Don't Miss You

I wanted to be in you
Not just sexually
But in every way
My body could attach to you

-I don't miss you I just think about you and what we could've been

Collage Me

I'm starting
to think
I'm more of a
collage
Then my relationships will ever be.

The Wrong Thing

You know what I realized since living in Brem?
All the time i'd wished for a guy
to be 100%
about me
to flaunt me
to show up for me
to support me and love every ounce of me

I realized i got what i wanted.

In every guy whom i dated,

was what i wanted them to be.
And that's great.
It's honestly so wonderful i was even capable of attracting exactly
What i wished

But,
You know what I've realized since living in Brem?

i was wishing for the wrong thing.
i should've been wishing
for someone whom *I* love
someone whom *I* support
someone whom *I* want to flaunt and flirt with and desire to be

I realized this
Because
To them
i was the girl of their dreams,
but to Me,
They were wish fulfillments
From wishing for the wrong thing

Too Much?

Is it too much to ask?
that I want to be
Surprised by you every visit

Is it too much to ask?
that I want to be
presented with flowers, bouquets
{even just one flower or even a petal will do}

Is it too much to ask?
that I want to be
picked up and twirled around every time you see me
{especially out in public like at a park or a zoo}

Is it too much to ask?
that I want to be
Kissed in the rain
Made out with at the gate of a plane

Is it too much to ask?
That you will (and that you want to) show up for me
when I need you most?

Is it too much to ask?
That you want to bring me little gifts
(things that not only made you think of me, but actually made you
want to show them to me)

Is it too much to ask?
That you can pick me up and twirl me around and give me a kiss

If this is too much to ask
Please leave.
Because my person would never not answer this wish

Energy Vampires

Okay, I plead
Energy vampires
Run away from me please

It's Interesting

It's interesting,
We never notice our spit
Until were cuddled on the couch
Anticipating to kiss

~ I'm more thoughtful about stuff like this

I Feel Like a Poem

I feel like a poem.
Like I am so poetic that everyone
Appreciates me
But most either are intimidated by me
Don't like me
Don't understand me
Or are in love with me.

What am I supposed to do with that?

<u>To Feel</u>

I feel happy
But not whole
Parts of me feel heavy
Parts of me feel
Woah.

Night Owl

You know why I'm a night owl?
Why it takes me so long to turn my phone off at night?
Why I stay up late until it's bright?
Because I think that by staying up an extra moment second minute hour
I may find the one
Who tells me to sleep tight
Who makes me want to go to bed
With me by their side at night

<u>Passenger Seat</u>

That passenger seat
side hug
Quick make out sesh
kind of love.
That's real. And I just witnessed it
through my apartment lobby window to the street
And I miss it.
Even though
I haven't really kissed it

Caffeine

I drank wayy too much caffeine today.

I kinda want to use this insanely buzzy heart speeding feeling to
let the crash exhaust me
to sleep.

Old Energy

How do I respond to him
After he just randomly texted me
To tell him I don't want to be
What he wants me to be — that I'm
Uncomfortable reconnecting— that I
Don't want to connect and
Exchange
old energy.

Routine

I miss the routine of waking up
Working out
Getting dressed
Eating breakfast
"Start the day with success"
Power afternoon
Errands ran
Bills paid
Boss called
Project done
Meal made
Face washed
Kinda day

I miss this.
Because what I do now is an inconsistent mess

It's time to get back to what I do best:
Dream giddy dreams
Paint flowers on my sleeves
And believe in magic
Fit for princesses and mice and kings

I just have to remember it takes a routine to become a queen.

Stained Glass

Today
I am not wearing
Pants. In fact,
I'm wearing
A thong. Yup.
Just a thong.
It is dark navy blue and has little cute cut outs
That look like pieces in a stained-glass window
And I love them.
And I love my butt cheeks on my back
-Very white in this Washington light-
But very loved
And soft and plump
And I love how my undies
Hug
The middle
And cup my sides
And give me something to pull up when I want to feel
Sexy
— I am in lingerie, right? —

I feel like stained glass light
;)

A Date

Write
Yourself a Love Note
Note everything
You love
To do
To be-
-Come with yourself
See what she sees-
Write Love inside her body
Head, veins, arms, legs, limbs
Walls
Walk with her
Take her on a date
Date that page, that letter, that note
Kiss her skin
Feel her lines, wrinkled edges, soft limbs
Heart beat steady
Right
Write a Love Note
Note what you love
To do -
-be determined to be
That body, that girl
Whose heart signs the page
Whose limbs, legs, arms, veins, head, whole body
take-
Took- her on a date.

Body Positivity

I am more body confident now
I often walk around my room
Naked
Makes me feel free
But walking
Around the house
Sitting on the couch
On the rug
Watching you —
Actually letting myself —
pore me something hot
In a mug
Pull myself into
A hug.

Snug as a bug in a rug.

I am more body confident now
I often walk about the house
Naked
By myself
{or sometimes with a skimpy little lingerie}
Makes me feel alive
I get a high like I can fly
Me to the moon
Electrify me
And watch every star twinkle shine glitter
I get the jitters
Up and down my mind
Through my hair
Down my spine
Along my chest heartbeat
Fast
Body positive breast.

Knowing everything about me
Makes me buzz.
To know everything about me my 1
I sometimes explore
The places where the sun doesn't shine
And when I do
I illuminate like the freaking sun
When it is that copper orange casted ball
Warm and hot and zingy bright love magic
In & outside within me

Place my hand on mine
Oh babe, baby
I'm confident I am
Mine.

Chocolate Petals

I would like to be a full-bodied
Chocolate
luxurious in taste
Rich in feel
Playful on your Lips
Tongue tastebuds
Wanting another lick
Kind of scent.

A perfume that is light
But so
So Rich, so
So Sweet, so
so Fragrant [decadent] aromatic
But not like a flower— no
no floral hint.

Chocolate is a dangerous seductive
as a flower is a delicate sensitive.

Chocolate's devourableness, bingeableness
Squirts, drips scented love with every melt, sip, lick.

Flowers are to be spoken to sweetly, picked,
Gathered in vases watered, pampered.

Spray, dab a chocolate perfume on my neck
Melt—
Melt me—
Melt me over petals picked.
Watch me become full-bodied
Luxurious
Decadently Chocolate-rich.

I Can't Wait

I can't wait until you find the confidence
to dance around naked
alone in the house
with your dog on the couch
and your spouse
Looking at you
like you are crazy
but also
the most Beautiful
Wonderful
Radiant
Magnificent
Being
He ever did see.

What a Wonderful
Radiant Magnificent
Life
That would be.

I can't wait until you find the confidence
to be present in your skin
Alive in your flesh
In-tune with your head that is a bit
Full of nonsense
But the kind that wins you jeopardy
And aces the extra credit, fun-fact questions on
Every test.

I can't wait until you find the confidence
to connect your beautiful body and all of its' not-so-flat-enough
stomach and roundabout curves
To your inquisitive mind,
So that you can inspire a nation of strong women

To dance with you, naked
In this Wonderful,
Radiant,
Magnificent life

All of a Sudden

All of a sudden
I'm seriously thinking
about living out of a van
Quitting my job
Doing art
Traveling
Creating
Meeting
Bonding
Spending
seriously spending time with others
seriously spending time in places
who are different
that are different
but centered around beauty and that radiate peace
All of a sudden
I want to actually enjoy and embrace
Life
Suddenly
Like I have never seen

-the hippie in me

Tastebuds in Your Ears

I love
People's ears when they chew
It's like they are little Rabbits
baby Goats, Kids, tiny Rodents
Discovering something new
A tastebud or two

Hear me out
People like to chew
It's like they are kids
Tasting everything
Chewing everything their mouths never knew
Growing tastebuds where tastebuds never grew.

<u>Poetry</u>

It's interesting
I told my ex I would write a poetry book about him
But as soon as I started to write

Everything became about me

I Fell in Love

I fell in love today for the first time in my life.
Like ocean deep.
And I can't explain it other than
Immense, but stomach wrenching, frightening
Beautiful
Perfect
peace

How can I go out with others
While this has always been my missing
Piece?

<u>Power</u>

Would you lay naked with a stranger?
Because I think that I would
I think that I am confident enough now
In knowing this power was a stranger once,
too.

Hey, Prince Charming

Hey, Prince Charming
Will you try this shoe on, please?

I like you
and I became something complex (but beautiful,
and rough-edged, but smoothed)
when I remembered the slippers were still on my feet

So, just try it on for me
-I think it will fit-

Because it is magic
that brought us together
and I don't want to keep the mice waiting
on the time you and I
could spend
Together
-
If it doesn't fit
That's okay
I understand.
But at least then I know
you tried.

Old Energy II

Are you going to ask me on a date?
I asked him.
Because I want to know how to set my energetic spiritual physical mental
Boundaries
With you.

White

I wonder how it feels
to be the color

White

Reflecting all that

Light

I bet it's a lot of work
Because you can never show your

Dirt.

Blossoming Droplets

Although I wither at thy words
I blossom at the remembrance
Of one's love,
One's life.
Although I wither at thy meadows
I will linger beside the stream
And watch one's love,
One's life,
No longer a drop in the stream
But a drop in my heart.

Alive Again

I love conversations until 2am;
They make me feel alive again :)

Lucid Reverie

The time has come to lay my head
Dream giddy dreams of the man
The warrior of love
Keeper of my heart.
Although the gates have been closed,
No one to enter.
None to win.
May the key be lost for slumber.

I must close my eyes upon the hour
Give my body to the dark of night.
Sleep shall come.

I Want to Be a Weed

I don't want to be a sunflower anymore
Because everyone knows sunflowers
Everyone takes pictures of them and with them
Everyone eats their seeds
Everyone points them out
Because they know what they look like —
They know what they stand for —
They know what they seek.

I want to be a weed.

I want to be a
A pretty little flower that is short and grows only on the hidden spot
In the grass kind of covered by other weeds that is hard to reach
I want people to look for me like a clover with four leaves
I want people to be amazed that something so beautiful
Could Grow
there
I want people to be caught off guard at my Prescence when they see me —
At their inability to look away —
Their inability to leave without very carefully picking me and taking me
With them —
Like the most beautiful thing they have ever seen
Like the most surreal, breathtaking thing they have ever experienced
Like a gift they want to always keep.

I don't want to be a sunflower.

I want to be a weed.

Beary

Ten years later,
He still sleeps with me
And I make sure to kiss his forehead and little feet
But,
I don't hug him like I used to
I don't twirl him around like a kite in the sky or
Pretend that I'm holding his hand at night.

I just be.

I let us both be.
And I know he still loves me— and I, he—
But
What happened to the little girl I used to be?
What happened to the "bring him to every sleepover" part of me?
The late night snuggles and weekday cereal for breakfast on my lap kinda
me?

I would like to think I let him sleep— that would be easier I think—
But,
Part of me knows that's something I would never believe

What do you think, Beary?
You're as old as me.

More Than You Are

Always be more than you are.
Remember that flowers have roots
that spread deep and far
At least flowers grow after snow.
What if
all we had ever wanted was something so pure,
and one day
it came.
How wonderful would that day be.
I think this is how a flower must feel when it thinks
all the while of how it will bloom, and then
one day
it does

Beauty in Black

I've learned there is a lot of birth in darkness
And that's okay.
I like the color black.
But from this point on
I am calling the shots on what things can bring me darkness
Verses what things let my light shine.
I now manage what I reflect
Put a dimmer on
Or keep turned off inside
So I don't become a place so gravely dark
Where I can't see what beauty I have actually sparked.

Changes

I call you a butterfly, but you don't think I mean this,
But I see so much more of you than you know.
I see your true beauty— what's behind those delicate, stained-glass,
powerful wings.
It looks something like kind-heartedness
And strong-willedness
And mental fortitude
And self-acceptance

But you don't see it.

I call you a butterfly, but you don't think I mean this,
Because you think that something delicate means that it's fragile
And since its fragile that it must be breakable.
But, Kenz, a butterfly is not broken.
How could it fly if it were broken?

I call you a butterfly, because you don't think I mean this,
Because you think that stained glass is ugly and not as worthy
Because of the fact that it's stained.
But, Kenz, those stains are intentional.
Those stains are not stains at all.
They are like tattoos.
They are polka dots and a tiger's marks and the birds up and down
your tattooed arm.
And you love tattoos.
Because you love self-expression.

I call you a butterfly, but you don't think I mean this,
Because you don't think that you are powerful
But, Kenz, a butterfly flies 1,000s of miles to migrate and doesn't die
And migrations are a power entirely of their own.

I call you a butterfly because I mean it.

I admire you more than you know.
For all the rest of us, however delicate we may roam,
Shall never understand the metamorphosis you went through
That shattered your chrysalis
Stained your glass
And took your power back.

But it was a catalyst.
The rest of us might lose our ability to transform

But you were shot out
Determined to find a place that you created that made you feel safe
You were willing to step into your new body
To question the purpose of your new wings
And to try to fly— to realize you can fly—
to migrate to your true home.

That is your beauty.
You are a delicate, stained-glass, powerful butterfly that other creatures wish they knew
But, Kenz,
You were born a caterpillar
And all other creatures like lady bugs and beetles die,
but you, sweet butterfly, you change <3

-for my beautiful sister, Mackenzie

Intimacy

All I want is intimacy
But I have my walls up
According to my reiki
My forearm is bottled with all of my traumatic energy
and heart chakra is very much closed
But my throat chakra is open
Breathing and speaking

— at least I speak my truth —

Even if my heart is closed
I don't put up with guys who
Don't give a shit about me
When I'm not in their room

— I speak my truth —

And right now
I want affection
I want attention
I want long-lasting
Fairytale-ending emotion

The last thing I want
Is another karmic lesson.

— My honest truth —
But what do I do with my
walls?

What Others See in Me

I want to get to the point where I can fully see
what others see
in me.
-all of the good things I know I am, but that I want to be

Fans

I used to always sleep with a fan on
I thought I needed the sound on
The continuous round and round on
And on and on on
To blanket the word around me so that I could sleep

I used to need the white noise to breathe
I would hold my breath and hide under the covers so my thought monsters wouldn't find me and scare me
Like I scared my own self into thinking

I used to want the fan on because it was a comfort to me
When I wasn't at home it helped me belong in a place that wasn't me
To lie in a bed that wasn't made for me
Sheets that weren't bought and washed for me
The fan was a constant to me

In college, my dorms didn't have fans
And that scared me
The first night sleeping with my store-bought tabletop
rotating fan was necessary
But so scary
I wasn't ready
I felt tossed out in the world with nothing I knew and a fan that didn't know how to carry me to sleep

I never got used to that fan
Probably because my subconscious didn't want to

And after I graduated
I sold that black fan.

And in Bremerton I got a new fan
It served a purpose there to cool me

To circulate the air like it did to aerate my thoughts
Its breeze watched over me

Now in Seattle I have a ceiling fan again
But I don't like it.
I've used it only once, but I never used it since
Because stillness is seeping into my body like an illness
And the thought of a fan
Would blow that all away

But I know that's not the reality.
And I'm overthinking.

But I'm proud that
I don't have to rely on a fan anymore
It's freeing actually
And no longer freezing

Stillness it fine
as long as I make sure to keep moving other parts of my life :)

Giddy

It is nice to feel giddy again
I've been sad and in my head
Blaming my job for my problems — for my funk —
But it was really just my view on myself

I was way too hard on myself
I never gave myself enough credit for all that I have done

Frick this funk
I moved 3 times in 1 year —
No wonder
I am not satisfied —
I don't even have a silverware organizer
I just bought paper towels last week
My washer flooded a few days ago
My thermostat broke
Seattle city life is no joke
and underground parking lots under Safeway grocery stores are where
people who are homeless
go to smoke

No wonder I felt broke.

So, I feel giddy again
A boy I like sent me a Snapchat again :)

I've been flooded with
Support
The past few days
And I've been pushing myself to workout more
Like how I did
but normal (you know, not OCD)

For a while

My body was unwell — I
can only imagine that further fueled my funk —
I got covid for 10 days
1 month later my throat became sore, and my ear got infected
A telehealth doctor gave me antibiotics
And I found saline solution for my ear

My body slowly healed
And my mind began to not be so sad
And I finally appreciated what all I have done
where I have been

I'm trying a swim team again
And I'm nervous
But it will be good to be back in the pool
In the water again

I heard from him a few days back
He got service somewhere along the pacific coast
and that was nice
I got so many butterflies — I
get so many butterflies—
Thinking of a life with him

But Snapchat boy texted me again
He has brothers and wants to move back to NYC
Part of me wants to join him
To live up to my childhood dream and live in a loft and be famous
But it's only been 3 days of texting

And I made him (of all things) the reason to be giddy

-why can't I be giddy for me?

Life in Color

I think I would be okay if I lived only in color.
Because I am made of color.
My soul has been colored with every color known.
I have become a color of my own.

And that is beautiful.

The Slipper II

Cinderella taught me grace
Day after day
I have her to thank for giving me slippers
Because that act of faith is what molded me into who I am today

But I was raised in Neverland
and I have learned to not land for something sweet
only to be bit by a snake or stung by a bee
I have learned to spread my butterfly wings
And I have flown far—farther then I thought I could have
in such a short time—
And that humbles me
That makes me proud to see.

However, I wasn't birthed
Didn't break breathe blush better me
Just to beam

I didn't brace myself just to be beat

I was broken
And when I finally blossomed
I was able to explore all of the battered, beautiful parts of me

That is where I met myself, you see.
I collected the pieces of my heart and childhood that had blown a
little farther than I'd know, and I dipped them in mod podge and
patched them on my heart, wrapped them around it like the quilt my
grandma made with my t-shirts and memories swaddled around me

I don't ever want to lose those parts of me again.
I argue that those parts are the best peaces of me.

But I did take time to miss the old me.

The sex-crazed, 22-year-old, exploratory-phase me
To grieve the end of this cycle that kept birthing new pieces that would
just break and be cut up and then be buried in mod podge only to be
collaged back on to me.

I am thankful for this journey.
It changed me forever.
Now I see relationships for what they are, sex as a precious entity, and
me as a powerful young woman who has been strengthened by so much
tragedy and heartbreak and lonely, but born again like a phoenix from
her misery.

. . .

Growing up has been painfully beautiful.
It was a fairytale of me finally understanding that my happy ending
showed me that I will never be Cinderella
because her cinders washed away at the end of each day.
I'm not saying I'm permanently tainted
Just that I am now more realistic, more understanding, more careful
to not touch cinders
Because that was once a place of flames.
Even though I am a Pisces
and water in the form of tears and swimming pools and scorching hot
showers extinguishes me
I've still been burned too many times to be clean.

Cinderelly Cinderelly
You have helped me Cinderelly

Thank you for birthing and raising me.
Even though I will never be you, I will always be like you
For I have developed from an infant to a child to a teen to a young adult
to a queen
in the process of becoming beautifully me :)

14985172R00098